my first book of QUESTIONS AND ANSWERS about EARTH AND SPACE

Anita Ganeri and Rosie Greenwood

p

This is a Parragon Book
First published in 2001

Parragon
Queen Street House
4 Queen Street
Bath BA1 1HE, UK

Copyright © Parragon 2001

Produced by

David West ⚥ Children's Books
7 Princeton Court
55 Felsham Road
Putney
London SW15 1AZ

British Library Cataloguing-in-Publication
Data

A catalogue record for this book is
available from the British Library.

ISBN 0-75255-843-9

Printed in China

Designers
Aarti Parmar, Rob Shone, Fiona Thorne

Illustrators
Angela & Andrew Harland, Mike Lacey,
Sarah Lees, Gilly Marklew, Dud Moseley,
Geoff Pleasance, Sarah Smith,
Stephen Sweet, Mike Taylor
(SGA)
Ian Thompson

Cartoonist
Peter Wilks (SGA)

Editor
James Pickering

CONTENTS

IS THERE LIFE ON MARS?
and other questions
about space

28 Which planet has the widest rings?

29 Which is the windiest planet?

29 Which planet is lying on its side?

30 How many stars are there?

30 Why is our galaxy called the Milky Way?

31 Are all galaxies the same?

32 How big is a red giant?

32 How small is a white dwarf?

33 What is a supernova?

34 When did the Universe begin?

35 What shape is the Universe?

WHY DOES THE EARTH SHAKE? and other questions about planet Earth

38 How old is the Earth?

39 How big is the Earth?

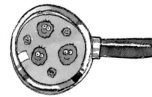

39 Where does the air stop?

40 What's under the ground?

40 Is the ground very thick?

41 What is a continent?

42 How do rocks change?

42 What are fire rocks?

43 Which rocks are made from shells?

44 What carves out caves?

44 What's the difference between stalagmites and stalactites?

45 Who explores caves?

46 How are mountains made?

46 Which is the highest mountain?

47 Do mountains shrink?

48 Why are some mountain tops snowy?

49 Where do you get rivers of ice?

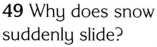

49 Why does snow suddenly slide?

50 Which mountains spit fire?

51 Why is lava runny?

51 Do people live near volcanoes?

52 Why does the Earth shake?

52 Are earthquakes dangerous?

53 Where do earthquakes happen?

54 Where do rivers start?

54 What is a spring?

55 What is a water cycle?

56 Which is the longest river?

56 How high are waterfalls?

57 How do rivers carve out valleys?

58 What makes a lake?

59 What is a reservoir?

59 Where is the world's biggest freshwater lake?

60 Which is the biggest island?

60 How are islands made?

61 Are new islands ever made?

62 What is sand made of?

62 Why do some beaches have cliffs?

63 What is the Giant's Causeway?

64 Why do we mine the Earth?

64 Where does oil come from?

65 Where do gemstones come from?

WHERE DO WAVES COME FROM? and other questions about oceans

68 How big is the sea?

68 Which is the biggest ocean?

69 Is an ocean the same as a sea?

70 Why is the sea salty?

70 Why is the sea blue?

71 Which sea has red sea water?

72 Where do waves come from?

73 Which waves roll as quickly as jet planes?

73 Who rides the waves?

74 What causes the tides?

74 What is the splash zone?

75 Are there rivers in the sea?

76 Is the sea bed flat?

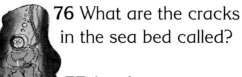

76 What are the cracks in the sea bed called?

77 Are there mountains underwater?

78 How deep is the sea?

78 Who made the deepest dive?

79 What are smokers?

80 Which fish glow in the dark?

80 What has got a big mouth?

81 What lives on the bottom of the ocean?

82 How does a coral reef grow?

82 Where do you find feathers, daisies and plates?

83 Where is the biggest coral reef?

84 Where do icebergs come from?

84 Is the Arctic too cold for animals?

85 Where is the Arctic Ocean?

86 Which animals live in the sea?

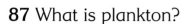

87 What is plankton?

88 How do people catch fish?

88 Who collects pearls?

89 Who drills into the sea bed?

90 Who studies shipwrecks?

91 Why do they need balloons?

91 Can shipwrecks be refloated?

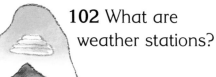

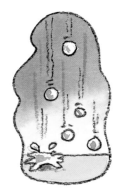
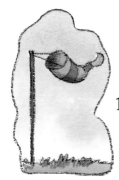

Is there life on Mars?

and other questions about space

?How many planets are there?

Our planet Earth is one of nine planets which travel around our star, the Sun – the scientific name for this round trip is an orbit. Nearly all of the planets have moons, which orbit them as they orbit the Sun. Other space bodies orbiting the Sun include mini-planets called asteroids. Together with the Sun, this family of planets, moons and other space bodies is called the Solar System.

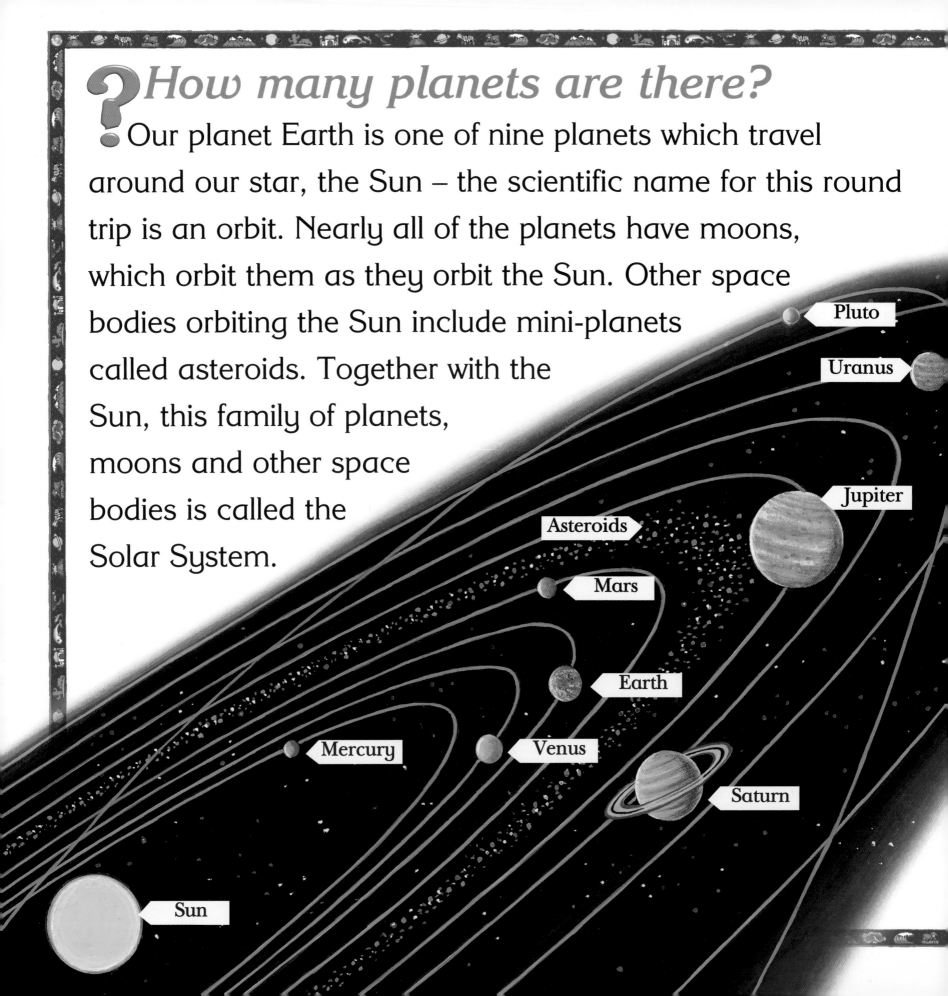

Pluto

Uranus

Jupiter

Asteroids

Mars

Earth

Mercury

Venus

Saturn

Sun

? How big is the Solar System?

Like just about everything else in space, the Solar System is huge. From one side to the other, it measures a mind-boggling 15,000 billion kilometres!

Neptune

? How old are the planets?

Scientists have worked out that the planets were born about 4.6 billion years ago. They formed from whirlpools of gas and dust, inside a massive doughnut-shaped cloud of gas and dust which was spinning around the Sun.

Which is the blue planet?

From space, Earth looks like a beautiful blue ball, with big patches of greeny-brown land and a swirling veil of white cloud. It's mostly blue, though, because nearly three-quarters of our planet's surface is covered in water – the oceans.

Why is the Earth special?

Earth is special because it's the only planet that we know has living things on it. Some of Earth's animals and plants could survive without breathing air, but none could live without water. Earth is the only planet in the Solar System to have plenty of liquid water on its surface – oceans full!

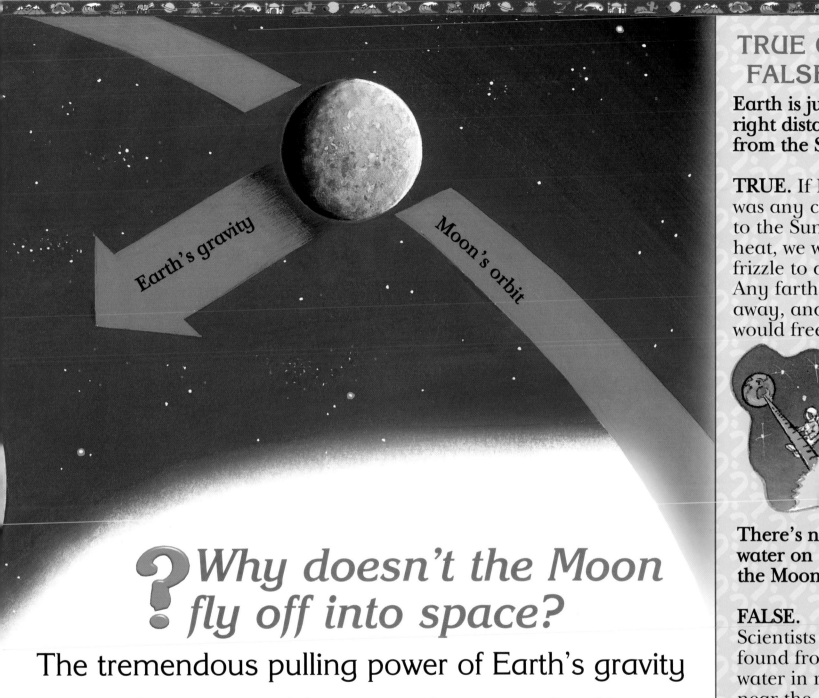

Earth's gravity

Moon's orbit

?Why doesn't the Moon fly off into space?

The tremendous pulling power of Earth's gravity works like an invisible string, keeping the Moon in its place. Everything in the Universe has gravity. The Sun's is so powerful that it stops Earth and all the other planets from flying away!

How big is the Sun?

The Sun is enormous! If the Sun were the size of a football, the Earth wouldn't be much bigger than this full stop. The Sun measures almost 1.4 million km across its middle.

6,000°C

15 million°C

What is the Sun made of?

Like all stars, the Sun is a vast glowing ball of fiery-hot gases. The two main gases in stars are called hydrogen and helium – they are the fuel supply for the stars' heat and light.

How hot is the Sun?

Even the coolest part of the Sun, its surface, is 6,000°C – 25 times hotter than the hottest kitchen oven. And the temperature soars to a scorching 15 million°C in the centre! The Sun is enormously bright, too. In fact, it shines so fiercely that even though Earth is millions of kilometres away, its light is strong enough to blind people. That's why you should never ever look at the Sun directly, even when you're wearing sunglasses.

NEVER LOOK AT THE SUN. IT IS VERY HARMFUL TO YOUR EYES.

?Where does the Sun go at night?

The Sun seems to vanish at sunset because the Earth is spinning around like a top as it orbits the Sun. One spin takes a whole day and night, and an orbit takes a year. Night happens when one half of the Earth spins out of the sunlight into darkness.

Earth spins from West to East.

?Why does the Moon shine?

Moons and planets aren't as big or as hot as stars, so they can't make light of their own. Our Moon shines because it works rather like a big mirror, reflecting the Sun's light down towards us.

Is there a man in the Moon?

No, although its surface sometimes looks like a big lumpy, bumpy face. The Moon is a dusty, lifeless desert, with no air or liquid water. It's covered in wide flat plains and high mountain ranges, and pitted with big hollows called craters, made by huge space rocks smashing into its surface.

The Moon is about a quarter the size of Earth.

TRUE OR FALSE?

The planets don't shine at night.

FALSE. They reflect the Sun's light, too. Venus looks brightest because it's the closest planet to the Earth.

Astronauts have landed on the Moon.

TRUE. American Neil Armstrong was the first, on 20 July, 1969.

Which planet has the biggest moons?

Gigantic Jupiter has the biggest moons. It has 16 moons in all, and three of them – Ganymede, Io and Callisto – are bigger than our Moon.

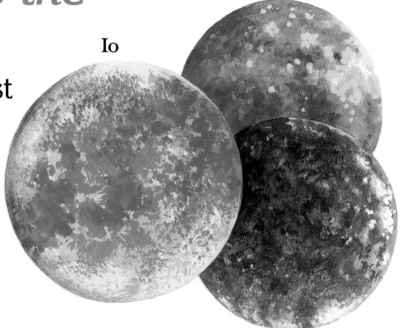

Io

Ganymede

Callisto

Phobos (left) and Deimos

Are all moons round?

The bigger ones are, but Mars's two tiny moons are potato-shaped. They're called Deimos and Phobos, and it would take you less than a day to walk across each of them. Our Moon is nearly 100 times wider than the pair of them joined together.

❓ *What is the difference between a planet and a moon?*

A moon is a space body that orbits a planet, while a planet is a space body that orbits a star like the Sun. Moons are smaller than their planet, while planets are smaller than their star!

Sun

Earth's orbit

Moon's orbit

? Are there snowballs in space?

Comets are rather like huge, dirty snowballs made of ice and rocky dust. Most of them stay far out towards the edge of the Solar System. Sometimes, however, a comet travels close enough to the Sun for the heat to boil its icy surface into a streaming tail of gas and dust.

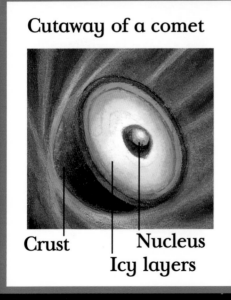

Cutaway of a comet

Crust

Nucleus

Icy layers

Shooting stars

? *What are shooting stars?*

The proper name for 'shooting stars' is 'meteors', and they aren't stars. Instead, they're pea-sized bits of space rock, burning up into dust as they plunge down through the air around the Earth. They look like fireworks streaking across the night sky.

? *Which planet orbits the Sun fastest?*

The closer a planet is to the Sun, the shorter and speedier its round trip. As the Sun's nearest neighbour, Mercury orbits once every 88 Earth-days – a lot zippier than Earth, whose orbit takes a year. The planet with the longest orbit is Pluto, the farthest from the Sun. Its orbit takes a massive 248 Earth-years!

Mercury

Pluto, the god of the underworld

Mars, the fiery god of war

Uranus was named after an Ancient Greek sky god

Saturn, the god of growth and farming

Jupiter, the king of the gods

Venus, the goddess of love

Neptune, the god of the sea

Mercury, the speedy messenger of the gods

❓ *How did the planets get their names?*

Most of the planets were named a long time ago, after the gods of the Ancient Romans.

? Which is the hottest planet?

Venus

If you think the closest planet to the Sun is the hottest, you're wrong! Venus can cook to a searing 500°C – nearly 1.5 times hotter than Mercury, and over 8 times hotter than the hottest place on Earth. Venus is such a scorcher because it's covered with thick clouds of heavy carbon dioxide gas, which work like a blanket holding in the heat. There's hardly any gas at all on Mercury, so there's nothing to stop the Sun's heat escaping.

Venus is covered in volcanoes.

TRUE. They all seem to have stopped erupting, but one of them is over 11 km high – 1.3 times as high as Mt Everest.

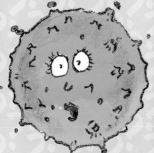

? *Which is the coldest planet?*

If you think the farthest planet from the Sun is the chilliest, you're right! Pluto is nearly 40 times as far from the Sun as Earth is, and temperatures there drop to a very icy minus 235°C – more than 2.5 times colder than the coldest place on Earth.

Pluto

Until 1930, no one knew Pluto was out there.

TRUE. It was the last planet to be found. Its moon, Charon, wasn't found until the 1970s.

Which is the red planet?

Mars

Mars is often called the red planet because much of its surface is covered in rusty-red sandy deserts. They aren't hot deserts, though – the temperature on Mars hardly ever rises above freezing point, even in summer.

Will people ever live on Mars?

There are plans to send astronauts there by 2020, to find out whether space bases can be built for scientists to live in and study Mars. So, who knows – maybe one day you will live on Mars yourself!

A space base may be built on Mars.

The Sojourner robot visited Mars in 1997.

?Is there life on Mars?

Scientists think that if any other planet in our Solar System ever had life on it, it was Mars. They aren't expecting to find green men or other big creatures, though. Instead, they hope to discover fossilised remains of microscopically tiny bacteria. But although spacecraft visited Mars in 1976 and 1997, and sent robots to hunt for fossils, they didn't find any trace of life.

TRUE OR FALSE?

Astronauts have set foot on other planets.

FALSE. The farthest any astronauts have travelled is the Moon.

There may be water on Mars.

TRUE. There are ice caps at Mars's north and south poles, which scientists think might contain frozen water.

Which is the biggest planet?

Jupiter

Jupiter is so big that all the other planets in the Solar System could squeeze inside it. Its Great Red Spot is a huge spinning storm that has been raging for 300 years, and it's big enough to swallow up two Earths!

What are the gas giants?

The planets Jupiter, Saturn, Uranus and Neptune are all big, and they're all mainly made of gas, which is why they're called gas giants. Unlike the other, rocky planets, the gas giants haven't got a solid surface. If a spacecraft tried to land on them, it would sink beneath the surface.

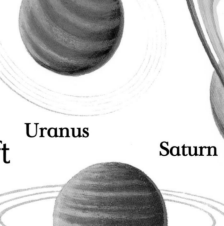

Jupiter

Uranus

Saturn

Neptune

Jupiter is as big as the Sun.

FALSE. Jupiter may be the biggest planet, but the Sun is nearly ten times wider.

Jupiter spins around more quickly than the other planets.

TRUE. Jupiter whirls around so quickly that its day and night lasts less than 10 Earth-hours.

❓ Which planets have rings?

All the gas giants have rings, which whirl around their middles rather like hula-hoops. The rings of Jupiter and Neptune are mainly made of space dust, but the rings of Saturn and Uranus are chunkier, with lumps of ice and rock in them.

Which planet has the widest rings?

More than 100 Earths would fit across Saturn's seven rings. Some people think that its spectacular, glistening rings make Saturn the most beautiful of the planets.

Saturn's rings

Storms on Neptune

? Which is the windiest planet?

Winds howl across Neptune's surface at over 2,000 kph. That's over six times faster than the most powerful hurricanes on Earth!

? Which planet is lying on its side?

Brilliant blue Uranus travels around the Sun on its side. Many scientists think that billions of years ago it bashed into another planet, which tipped it over.

Collision with Uranus

How many stars are there?

The Sun and all the stars that twinkle in the night sky belong to our huge star group, the Milky Way galaxy. There are about 1,000 billion stars in the Milky Way, and there are lots of other galaxies, too. Scientists think there are 100 billion billion stars in as many as 100 billion galaxies.

Why is our galaxy called the Milky Way?

The Milky Way got its name because we can sometimes see part of it at night, looking like a milky band of starlight stretching across the sky.

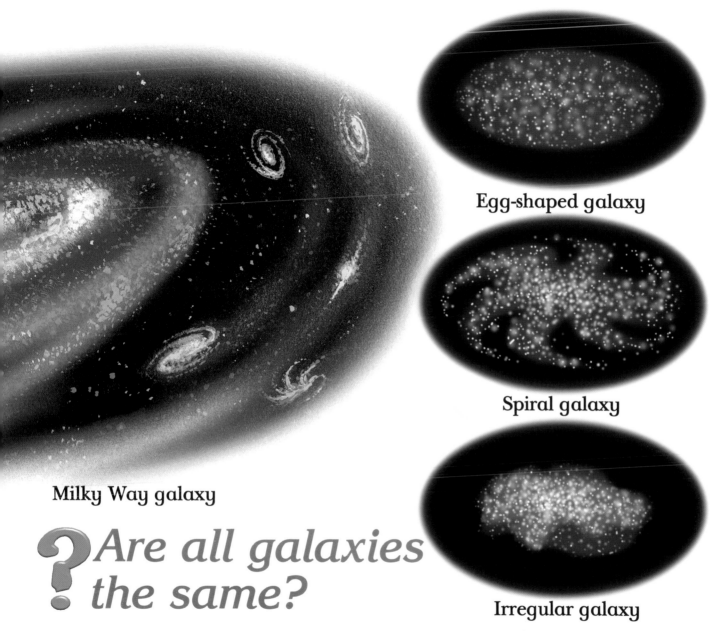

Milky Way galaxy

Egg-shaped galaxy

Spiral galaxy

Irregular galaxy

?*Are all galaxies the same?*

No, they come in three main shapes. Some are spirals like the Milky Way – it looks like a whirlpool from above, and like two fried eggs stuck together from the side. Others are egg-shaped or irregular (with no particular shape).

How big is a red giant?

After billions of years, all stars begin to run out of fuel. When this happens to medium-sized stars like our Sun, they swell up and can grow 100 times bigger. These vast stars are called red giants.

Red giant

Birth of a star

How small is a white dwarf?

After a red giant uses up all its gas fuel, it shrinks to as much as 10,000 times smaller. This is a white dwarf, and although it's small it's still very hot.

❓ *What is a supernova?*

Not all stars die quietly. Some are much bigger than our Sun, with a lot more fuel. The more massive the star, the shorter its life and the faster its death. The very biggest stars go out with a bang, in an explosion called a supernova.

White dwarf

Supernova

When did the Universe begin?

The Universe is everything – you, the Earth and everything on it, the Sun and the Solar System, the Milky Way and all the other galaxies. And scientists think it all began about 15 billion years ago, with a huge explosion they call the Big Bang.

Big Bang

The Universe is still getting bigger.

❓ *What shape is the Universe?*

For many years people thought the Universe was round, like a blown-up balloon. But some scientists now think it might be flattish – like a pancake!

The Universe may be pancake-shaped.

Why does the Earth shake?

and other questions about planet Earth

How old is the Earth?

Scientists think the Earth formed about 4.6 billion years ago – a very long time indeed! It was made from a giant cloud of hot gas and dust which shrank and cooled to make a huge ball. The Earth isn't perfectly round, though. It bulges out in the middle and is slightly squashed at the top and bottom.

Earth seen from space

How big is the Earth?

The Earth is enormous! It measures 40,075 km around the equator which is the fattest part of the Earth. It measures about 40,000 km around the Poles. The Earth weighs a whopping 6,000 million million million tonnes.

Where does the air stop?

There is an invisible blanket of air around the Earth. It's called the atmosphere. The air reaches up for about 500 km above your head. This is where the air stops and space begins.

Space

Upper atmosphere

500 km

Earth's surface

❓ What's under the ground?

The ground is made of hard rock. Underneath are more layers of rock and metal. Some of these layers are so hot they've melted and gone runny.

❓ Is the ground very thick?

Yes, it is! However hard you jump up and down, you won't fall through! The rocky ground is called the Earth's crust. It's about 40 km thick on dry land and about 8 km thick underneath the sea.

Continent

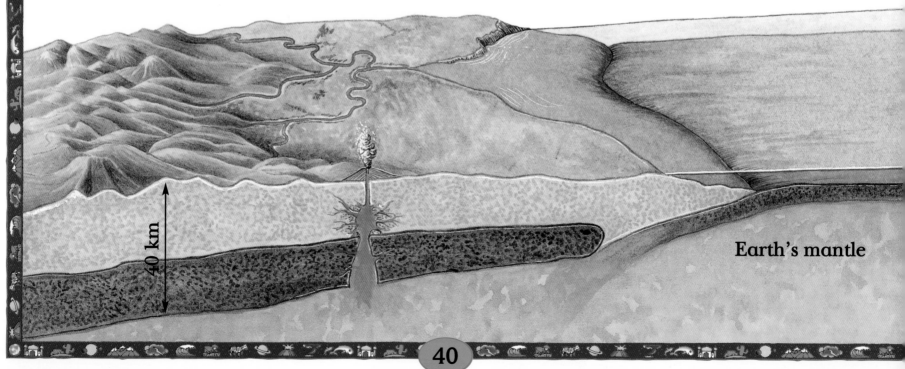

40 km

Earth's mantle

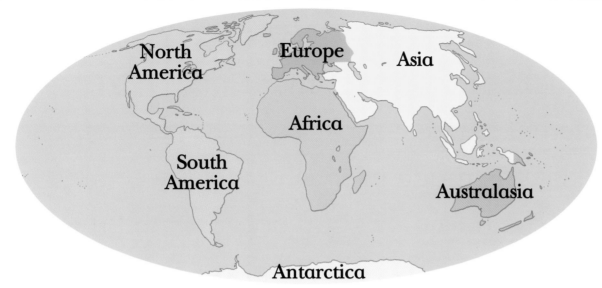

North America

Europe

Asia

Africa

South America

Australasia

Antarctica

?*What is a continent?*

The Earth's crust is cracked into seven pieces called continents. Starting with the biggest, they are Asia, Africa, North America, South America, Antarctica, Europe and Australasia.

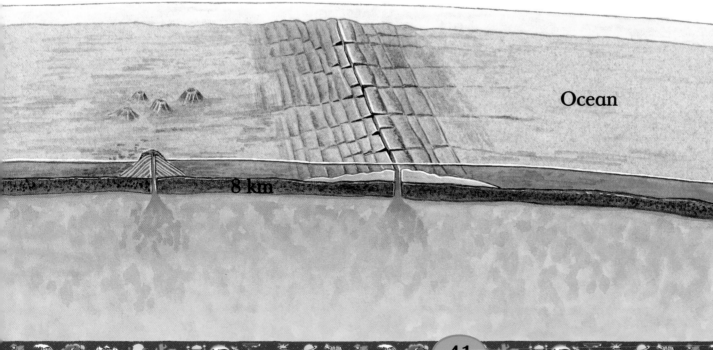

Ocean

8 km

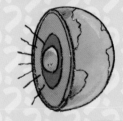

? *How do rocks change?*

The Earth's crust is made of different kinds of rock. Each kind is made in a different way. Some rock is pushed underground, where the rock is heated and squeezed. It changes into a different rock called metamorphic rock.

Marble

Lava (liquid rock) cools to form IGNEOUS rock.

Rock around magma (underground liquid rock) is changed by heat to form METAMORPHIC rock.

Rocks are squeezed and folded to form METAMORPHIC rock.

? *What are fire rocks?*

Fire rocks are also called igneous rocks. They are made deep inside the Earth, when hot, melted rocks cool and harden. Igneous rocks shoot out of volcanoes when they erupt.

Pumice

Rocks are broken down by wind, rain and ice, and carried away by rivers.

? *Which rocks are made from shells?*

Some rocks are made from tiny grains of rock squashed together in layers. This is called sedimentary rock. It sometimes contains fossil plants and animals. Chalk is a kind of sedimentary rock. It is made from the shells of tiny sea creatures that lived millions of years ago.

Tiny creatures living in the sea millions of years ago sink to the sea bed.

Chalk

Sediment from the river forms layers of new rock called SEDIMENTARY rock.

Rivers carry small particles of rock called sediment to the sea.

? What carves out caves?

When rainwater trickles through a crack in the ground, it eats away at the rocks below. This carves out underground caves and tunnels. Some caves are enormous, big enough to fit a huge cathedral inside.

? What's the difference between stalagmites and stalactites?

Stalagmites and stalactites are long and pointed, like rocky icicles. But stalagmites grow up from the floor and stalactites grow down from the ceiling.

Stalagmite

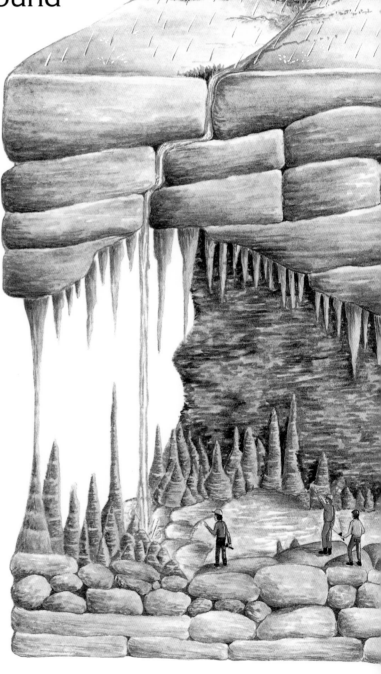

? Who explores caves?

People who like to explore caves and tunnels are called potholers. They climb down on ropes or ladders. It's dark, wet and cold underground. The potholers wear warm, waterproof clothes and carry torches so they can see.

Potholers exploring an underground cave

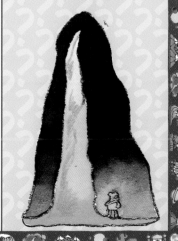

How are mountains made?

Some mountains are made when two pieces of the Earth's crust crash into each other. They push the rock in between into giant folds. Other mountains are made when huge blocks of rock are pushed up.

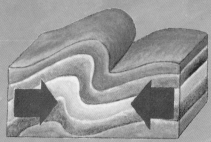

Fold mountain

Block mountain

Which is the highest mountain?

The highest mountain in the world is mighty Mt Everest in Asia. It is 8,848 m tall. It is part of a range of towering mountains called the Himalayas.

Peak of Mt Everest

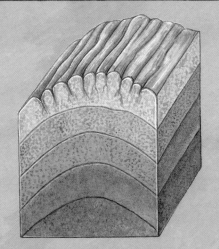
Top layer cracks.

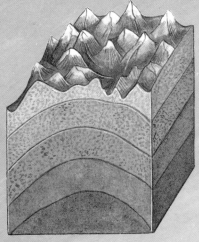
Wind, rain and ice wear down rock.

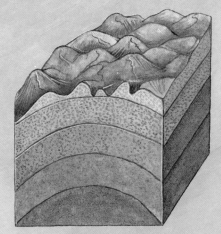
Mountains continue to wear down.

❓Do mountains shrink?

Mountains take millions of years to grow. But they're getting smaller every day. The mountains are battered by wind, frost and ice which break off tiny chips of rock and carry them away. Young mountains have sharp, pointed peaks. Older mountains are smoother and rounder.

❓ *Why are some mountain tops snowy?*

The higher you climb up a mountain, the colder it gets. At the very top of a high mountain, it's freezing cold and the ice and snow never melt. Lower down, it's warmer, and trees and plants can grow.

Animals that live high up on mountains have thick, woolly coats to keep them warm. Mountaineers must wear special clothes.

Snow and ice

Alpine meadows

Coniferous forest

Deciduous forest

Glaciers

?Where do you get rivers of ice?

Glaciers are giant rivers of ice which slide down mountain slopes. They begin high up when snow collects in a dip in the rock. The snow hardens and turns to ice, which slides downhill. Rocks and stones stuck in the ice scrape away at the rocks and carve out deep valleys.

?Why does snow suddenly slide?

Sometimes a huge mass of snow suddenly breaks loose and crashes down a mountain. This is called an avalanche. The snow races along faster than an express train and buries any people or houses in its path.

Layers of snow and ice

Avalanche

TRUE OR FALSE?

Glaciers flow like rivers.

TRUE. Glaciers flow downhill like rivers. But they usually flow slowly, at just a few centimetres each day.

Singing can set off an avalanche.

TRUE. Loud singing really can set off an avalanche. In some mountain villages, singing is banned.

❓ *Which mountains spit fire?*

Volcanoes are mountains that spit out burning ash, gas and liquid rock. The ash and rock come from deep under the ground. They burst up through cracks in the Earth's crust. Some volcanoes erupt quietly. Others explode with a loud bang.

Burning ash

Liquid rock (lava)

Why is lava runny?

The hot, runny rock that comes out of a volcano is called lava. It is thick and sticky, like treacle. As it cools in the air, it turns into rock.

Volcanic lava

Do people live near volcanoes?

Many people live near volcanoes even though it's a dangerous thing to do. The ash that shoots out of a volcano makes the soil very rich and perfect for growing crops in.

Why does the Earth shake?

The pieces of rock which make the Earth's crust, drift on the hot, runny rock beneath. Sometimes two pieces push against each other. Suddenly the rocks jerk apart and make the ground shake in an earthquake.

Fault

Pressure builds as Earth moves.

The two parts spring apart.

Are earthquakes dangerous?

Big earthquakes are very dangerous. Cracks appear in the ground and buildings and bridges topple over. Many people may be injured or killed, or lose their homes.

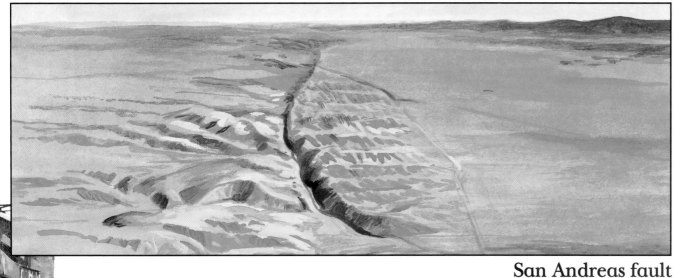

San Andreas fault

❓ *Where do earthquakes happen?*

Many earthquakes happen where two pieces of crust meet. These places are called faults. The city of San Francisco in the USA sits on the San Andreas Fault. It has hundreds of earthquakes a year.

TRUE OR FALSE?

Dogs howl before an earthquake.

TRUE. It's also said that rats run away in panic and goldfish even jump out of their bowls!

Earthquakes last for hours.

FALSE. Most earthquakes last for less than a minute. The longest earthquake ever felt lasted for four minutes.

Where do rivers start?

Many rivers begin high up on mountains as tiny streams. Others trickle out of lakes or flow from the ends of glaciers as they start to melt.

Mountains

Glacier

Lake

Tributary

Spring

What is a spring?

Some rivers start off as springs bubbling up out of the ground. A spring spurts up when rainwater seeps underground, then gushes back up to the surface again.

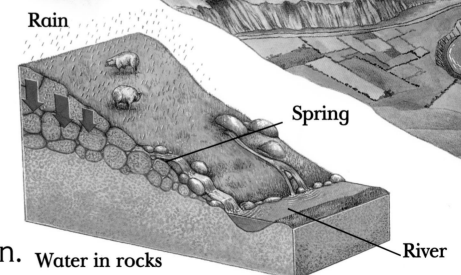

Rain

Spring

River

Water in rocks

Rainfall

Cloud blown over land

Water returns back to sea in rivers.

Evaporation

?*What is a water cycle?*

Rivers carry water into the sea. The Sun heats the sea and millions of litres of water evaporate as invisible water vapour. It cools to make clouds, then rain falls from the clouds back into the rivers.

? Which is the longest river?

The longest river is the River Nile in Egypt. It flows for 6,695 km. But the biggest river is the River Amazon in South America. It carries 60 times more water than the Nile – about a fifth of all the river water on Earth.

? How high are waterfalls?

The world's highest waterfall is Angel Falls in Venezuela, South America. The water splashes 979 m down a tall mountainside. Waterfalls happen when a river flows over a ledge of hard rock. The water eats away at the soft rock below and carves out a steep cliff.

Angel Falls

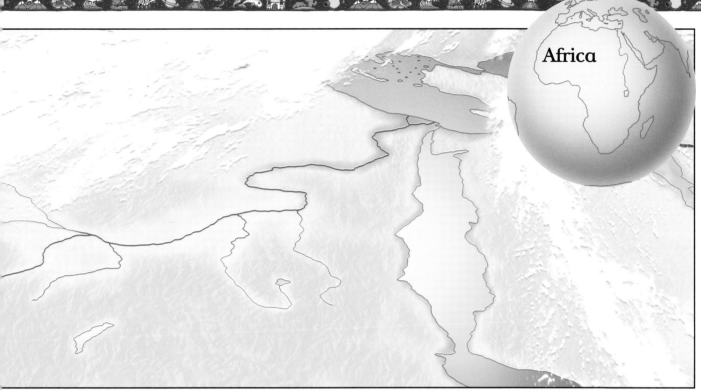
Africa

River Nile seen from space

River valley, Grand Canyon USA

? How do rivers carve out valleys?

As a river flows downhill, it carries lots of rough rocks and stones. These scrape away at the riverbed and its sides, carving out deep valleys over many years.

TRUE OR FALSE?

The D River is the shortest river on Earth.

TRUE. The D River in Oregon, USA, is just 37 m long. The River Nile is about 180,000 times longer!

Some rivers flow underground.

TRUE. Rainwater trickles under the ground and fills up rivers. But not many people have ever seen them.

57

What makes a lake?

Some lakes form in dips in the ground, scraped out by ice. They fill with rainwater to make a lake. Some lakes are made when a river cuts through a bend. Other lakes form in volcanoes when the crater fills up with water.

Rainfall fills up cone of volcano.

Depression in landscape creates a lake where it falls below the water level in the surrounding rock.

Oxbow lake is formed by river rejoining itself.

River

Valley before

Reservoir

Valley after dam is built.

? What is a reservoir?

A reservoir is a lake which is used for storing water. The water is used for drinking and making electricity. To make a reservoir, people build a dam to stop the water flowing.

? Where is the world's biggest freshwater lake?

The biggest freshwater lake is Lake Superior in North America. It covers 82,100 square kilometres. At 1.6 km deep, Lake Baikal in Siberia is the deepest.

Lake Baikal

Which is the biggest island?

Greenland

If you count Australia as a continent, the biggest island is Greenland in the icy Arctic Ocean. It covers 2,175,000 square kilometres, nine times the area of Britain.

How are islands made?

An island is a chunk of land which has water all around it. Some islands have broken off continents or have been cut off by the sea. Some are the tops of volcanoes which grow under the sea.

Sea level rises to create islands which were originally part of the mainland.

Old sea level

Surtsey

?Are new islands ever made?

Yes, they are! In 1963, a new island appeared near Iceland. It was made by a volcano erupting under the sea. The island was named Surtsey, after an ancient god of fire.

Volcanoes rise above the surface to create islands.

TRUE OR FALSE?

Some islands are made of coral.

TRUE. Many tiny islands in the Pacific and Indian Oceans are made of ancient coral reefs.

New York City is built on an island.

TRUE. Most of the city of New York in the USA is built on an island called Manhattan.

What is sand made of?

Sand is made of small chips of rock and seashell. The wind and rain break the rocks up. The waves wash the shells on to the beach and smash them into tiny pieces.

Why do some beaches have cliffs?

As waves crash on to the shore, they change the shape of the coastline. The water carves out cliffs, caves and arches in the rocks along the shore. Sometimes, the middle of an arch collapses and leaves a stack of rock behind.

Stacks

Arch

9865

Giant's Causeway

❓What is the Giant's Causeway?

The Giant's Causeway in Northern Ireland is made of hundreds of rocky blocks and pillars along the coast. The rocks came from an ancient volcano. A story says that giants used the causeway to cross the sea to Scotland.

TRUE OR FALSE?

Some cliffs are made of chalk.

TRUE. Some cliffs are made of soft, white chalk. You can sometimes find the fossils of seashells in them.

Beaches can disappear overnight.

TRUE. Rough seas and violent weather can batter beaches, sweeping them into the sea.

❓ Why do we mine the Earth?

There are lots of useful things underground, including coal, metals and gemstones. To get them out, people dig deep pits called mines.

Oil rig

❓ Where does oil come from?

Oil is made from tiny prehistoric plants and sea animals. Their bodies sank to the sea bed and were covered by layers of sand and mud. Over millions of years, they turned into oil. People drill holes and pump the oil out.

Emerald gemstone

Where do gemstones come from?

Gemstones grow in the rocks of the Earth's crust. Some, such as diamonds, sapphires and emeralds, are very rare and precious. They are dug out of the ground, cut and polished. Then they're made into beautiful jewellery.

Where do waves come from?

and other questions about oceans

How big is the sea?

The sea is absolutely huge! In fact, sea water covers two thirds of the Earth – that's twice as much as land does. The sea is made up of five oceans. They are the Pacific, the Atlantic, the Indian, the Southern and the Arctic.

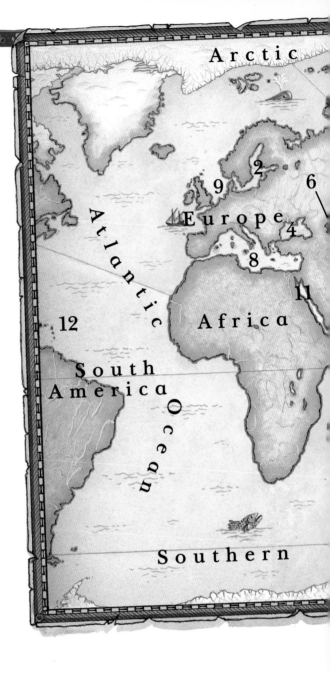

Which is the biggest ocean?

The biggest ocean by far is the Pacific Ocean. It covers about a third of the Earth and stretches halfway around the world. All the land on Earth would fit into it, with room to spare. The Pacific is also much deeper than the other oceans.

Pacific Ocean

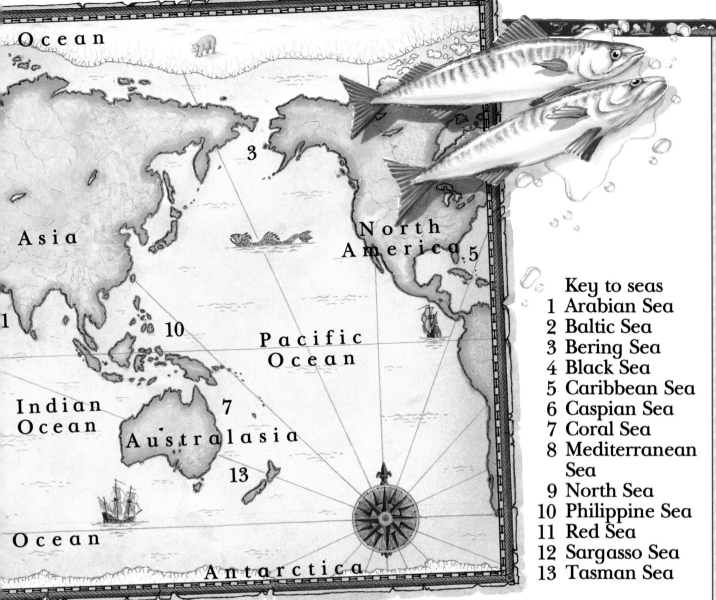

Ocean

Asia

North
America 5

1

10

Pacific
Ocean

Indian
Ocean

7

Australasia

13

Ocean

Antarctica

Key to seas
1 Arabian Sea
2 Baltic Sea
3 Bering Sea
4 Black Sea
5 Caribbean Sea
6 Caspian Sea
7 Coral Sea
8 Mediterranean Sea
9 North Sea
10 Philippine Sea
11 Red Sea
12 Sargasso Sea
13 Tasman Sea

❓*Is an ocean the same as a sea?*

Many people use the words ocean and sea to mean exactly the same thing. But scientists who study the oceans say they are different. They say a sea is a particular part of an ocean which has its own name.

? Why is the sea salty?

The sea is salty because it has so much salt in it. It's the same sort of salt you sprinkle on your food. Most of the salt comes from the land. The rain washes it out of rocks and carries it to the sea.

? Why is the sea blue?

On a sunny day, the sea looks blue. This is because it reflects blue light rays from the Sun. On a cloudy day, the sea looks grey because the clouds hide the Sun.

Collecting sea salt

❓ *Which sea has red sea water?*

In summer the water of the Red Sea looks pinkish-red. Millions of tiny red plants called algae grow in the sea and change the colour of the water. The Red Sea has the saltiest sea water in the world.

Red Sea

TRUE OR FALSE?

Sea water is good to drink.

FALSE. Sea water is so salty it tastes horrible. It can make you sick if you drink it.

The Black Sea is very dirty.

FALSE. The Black Sea gets its name because it's full of thick, black mud.

Where do waves come from?

Waves are ripples of water made by the wind blowing across the surface of the sea. On calm days, the waves are small. But on windy days, they grow bigger and bigger until their tops tip over and they crash on to the shore.

Tsunami

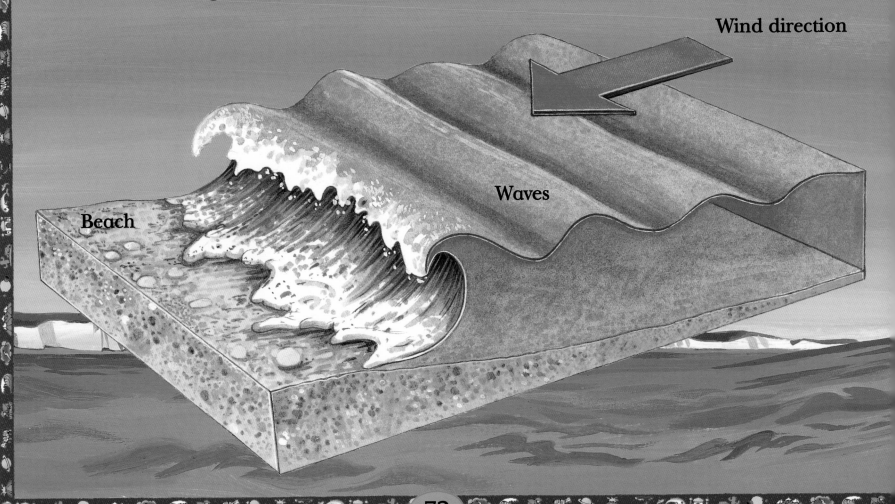

Wind direction

Waves

Beach

Which waves roll as quickly as jet planes?

Tsunamis (soo-nam-ees) are giant waves. They are caused when earthquakes shake the sea bed or a volcano erupts under the sea. They race through the sea as quickly as a jet plane, rear up and drown the land.

Who rides the waves?

Surfers love to ride the waves and the bigger the waves, the better. Some waves in Hawaii are five times taller than the surfers themselves.

What causes the tides?

Twice a day, the sea rolls high up on to the beach, then it flows back out again. The tides are caused by the Moon and Sun pulling the sea into giant bulges on either side of the Earth. It's a bit like water sloshing to and fro in a giant bowl.

What is the splash zone?

The splash zone is part of the beach that is splashed with water as the tide comes in. Animals such as limpets have to cling tightly to the rocks so they're not washed out to sea.

Are there rivers in the sea?

Currents are giant bands of water that flow through the sea like rivers, blown by the wind. Currents can carry hot or cold water. As they flow around the world, they help to heat and cool the Earth. The biggest current is the West Wind Drift around Antarctica. It carries 2,000 times more water than the mighty River Amazon.

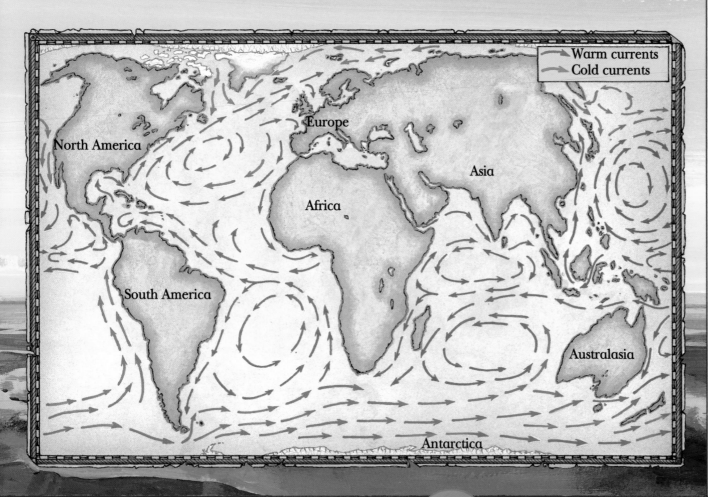

Warm currents
Cold currents

North America

Europe

Asia

Africa

South America

Australasia

Antarctica

Is the sea bed flat?

About half of the sea bed is very flat and covered in huge, smooth plains. But the rest isn't flat at all. There are deep valleys, high mountains and volcanoes under the sea, just as there are on land. The only difference is that you can't see them!

What are the cracks in the sea bed called?

They're called trenches, and some are over 10 km deep. Trenches are made when one piece of sea bed crashes into another and is pushed underneath it.

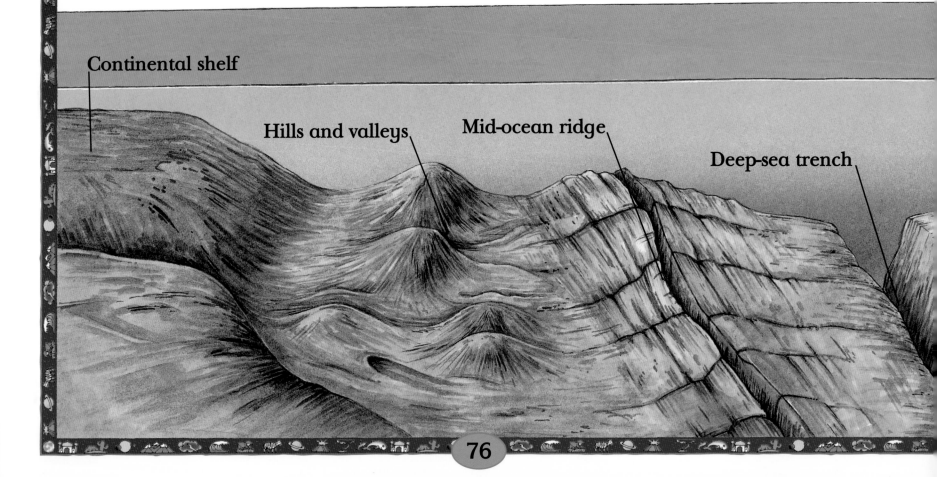

Continental shelf

Hills and valleys

Mid-ocean ridge

Deep-sea trench

?Are there mountains underwater?

There are thousands of mountains under the sea. They're all volcanoes, though they don't all erupt anymore. A long line of mountains stretches all the way down the Atlantic Ocean. It's called the Mid-Atlantic Ridge, and it's the longest chain of mountains in the world. The highest sea mountains are over 10,000 m tall.

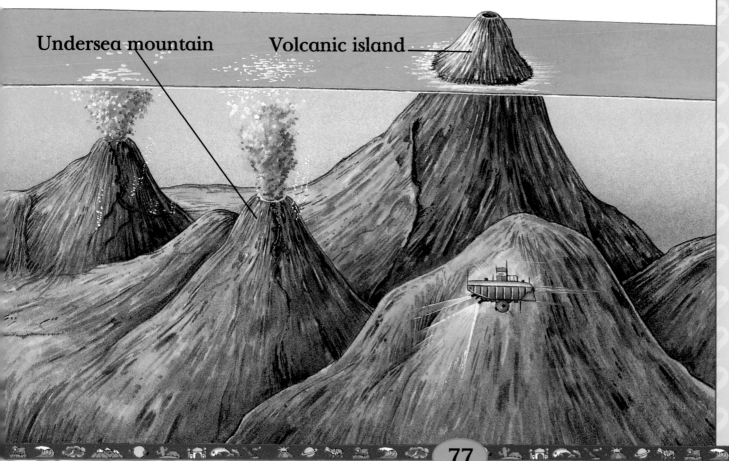

Undersea mountain   Volcanic island

TRUE OR FALSE?

Some mountains poke out of the water.

TRUE. Some underwater mountains are so tall, their tops stick out of the sea and make islands.

Continents have shelves.

TRUE. Along the coast, the land slopes gently into the sea. This is called the continental shelf.

How deep is the sea?

The deepest part of the sea is the Marianas Trench in the Pacific Ocean. Here the sea plunges to more than 11 km. That's deep enough to swallow Mt Everest, the highest mountain on Earth, with plenty of room to spare.

Trieste

Who made the deepest dive?

In 1960, two men dived almost to the bottom of the Marianas Trench inside the submersible Trieste. A submersible is like a small submarine. The dive took about 5 hours. Trieste was very strong to stop the men being crushed by the water.

❓ *What are smokers?*

❓ Deep down in the Pacific Ocean, fountains of scalding hot water gush up out of cracks in the sea bed. Chemicals in the hot water colour the water black. Some of the chemicals sink down and build tall chimney stacks around the cracks. These are called smokers because the black water looks like smoke billowing out of a chimney.

Which fish glow in the dark?

Angler fish

It's inky black in the deep sea, so many deep-sea fish make their own lights. Flashlight fish have lights under each eye. They use their lights to help them find food and can blink the lights on and off.

Gulper eel

What has got a big mouth?

Food is hard to find in the deep sea so fish have to make the most of a meal. Gulper eels have very big mouths and stretchy stomachs for swallowing large mouthfuls of food.

Starfish

Tripod fish

? What lives on the bottom of the ocean?

The deep sea is dark and freezing cold. Even so, it's home to thousands of fish and other creatures. Deep-sea fish and squid swim in the water. Starfish, sea urchins, sponges and strange, sausage-like sea cucumbers live on the sea bed.

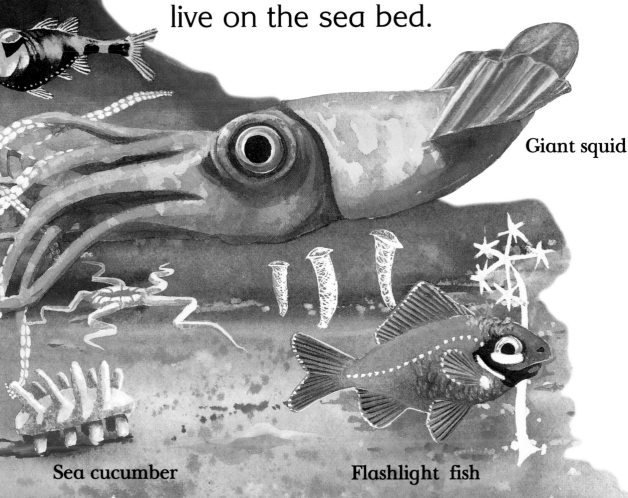

Giant squid

Sea cucumber

Flashlight fish

TRUE OR FALSE?

Angler fish use fishing rods.

TRUE. Angler fish use a long fin with a blob of light on the end to fish for their food.

Some fish have legs.

FALSE. Fish don't really have legs but the tripod fish has three extra-long fins for standing on the sea bed.

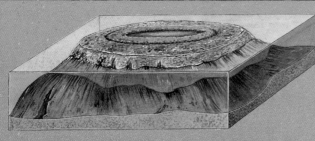

Coral grows in warm, shallow water around coastlines.

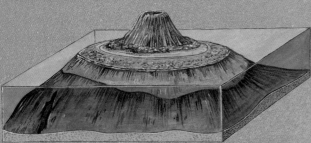

Even when an island sinks below the surface or the sea level rises the coral keeps growing.

? How does a coral reef grow?

Coral reefs are made by millions of tiny sea animals. They make hard skeletons around their soft bodies. When they die, the skeletons are left behind, and slowly build up the reef.

? Where do you find feathers, daisies and plates?

On a coral reef! They are all types of coral which look like feathers, daisies or dinner plates. Other types of coral look like tiny trees or a deer's antlers. Some even look like brains. Brain corals can grow to more than 2 m across.

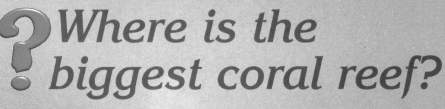

Where is the biggest coral reef?

The biggest coral reef in the world grows off the north-east coast of Australia. It stretches for more than 2,000 km and is called the Great Barrier Reef. The reef is incredibly old. It began to grow about 18 million years ago.

Australia

Great Barrier Reef

TRUE OR FALSE?

You can see the Great Barrier Reef from space.

TRUE. The Great Barrier Reef is so big, astronauts can see it from space.

Parrots live in the sea.

FALSE. Real parrots don't live in the sea but parrot fish do. These parrots eat coral.

Where do icebergs come from?

Icebergs are huge chunks of ice that break off the ends of glaciers or ice sheets. They float in the sea until they melt. Only the tip of an iceberg shows above water. The rest is hidden under the sea. This makes them very dangerous to ships.

Arctic tern

Walrus

Killer whale

Narwhal

Is the Arctic too cold for animals?

The Arctic Ocean is icy cold but it is home to many animals. Giant whales live in the sea, and polar bears roam across the ice and hunt seals. Arctic terns and other birds are summer visitors.

Where is the Arctic Ocean?

The Arctic Ocean is in the far north, at the very top of the world. It is the smallest ocean and for most of the year, it's covered in thick ice. The North Pole is in the middle of the Arctic Ocean.

Polar bear

Beluga

Great right whale

North America

North Pole.

Arctic Ocean

Northern Asia

Which animals live in the sea?

You'll find a huge number of animals living in the sea. There are huge sharks, speedy sailfish, seals, squid, turtles, prawns, whales, octopuses, and many more. You can see some of them below. Most animals live in the top part of the sea where the water is warm.

Albatross

Great white shark

Seal

Marlin

Moray eel

Tuna

Shrimp

Octopus

Dolphin fish

Squid

What is plankton?

Billions of tiny plants and animals live near the surface of the sea. They're called plankton. Without plankton, sea creatures would have nothing to eat. Fish eat the plankton, then they're eaten by bigger fish and other animals, such as seals and whales.

Plankton

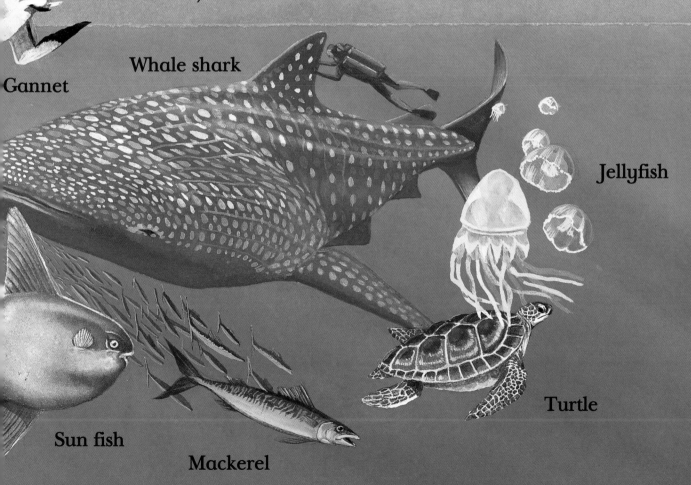

Gannet

Whale shark

Jellyfish

Sun fish

Mackerel

Turtle

How do people catch fish?

Some fishermen use simple rods and lines, spears, traps and pots to catch fish. Others use huge nets dragged through the water by boats called trawlers. Some modern fishing boats clean and freeze the fish on board, so they can stay at sea for weeks.

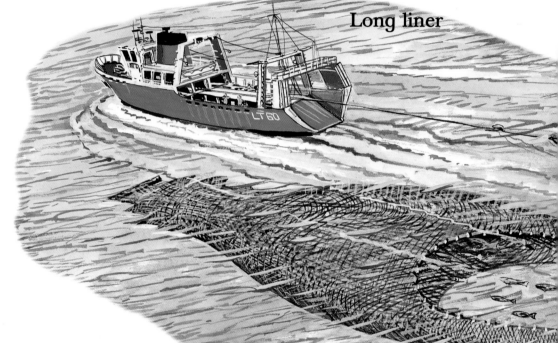

Long liner

Lobster fishing boat

Who collects pearls?

Some people risk their lives diving for pearls, which grow inside the shells of oysters, mussels and clams. They're very rare and valuable. The biggest pearl ever found was the size of a football.

？ *Who drills into the sea bed?*

People drill into the sea bed to find oil. Oil is made from the bodies of tiny prehistoric plants and animals. They sank and were covered by sand and mud. Over millions of years, they turned into oil.

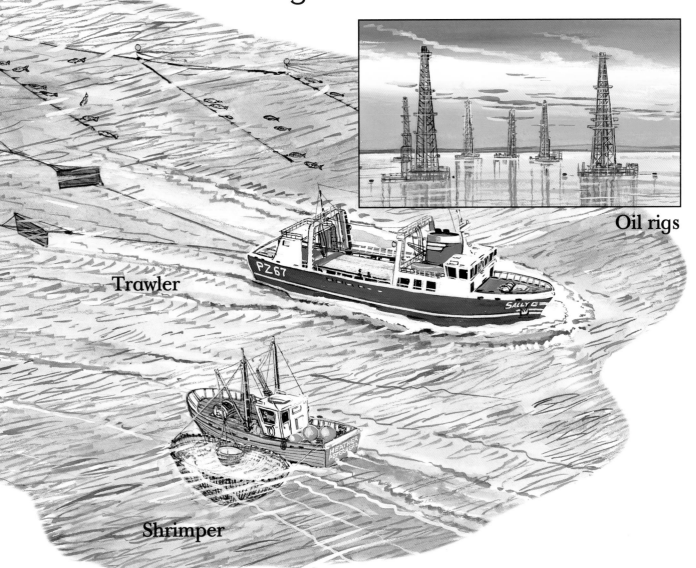

Oil rigs

Trawler

Shrimper

Who studies shipwrecks?

Archaeologists are people who find out what life was like long ago by looking at ancient objects and ruins. Some archaeologists study shipwrecks deep beneath the sea. They dive and look for clues, such as coins, clothes and cargo, and precious treasure, such as gold and silver.

?Why do they need balloons?

It can be difficult to move some of the objects, especially if they're fragile or heavy. So archaeologists put them in a box and fix it to an air-filled bag which looks like a balloon. The balloon floats to the surface, lifting the box with it.

?Can shipwrecks be refloated?

Yes, they can. In 1961, the wreck of the warship Wasa was brought to the surface. It is now in a museum in Stockholm, Sweden. The ship sank in Stockholm harbour in 1628. Two floating cranes helped to lift it out of the sea.

❓ *Who wears a special suit?*

Divers have to wear special diving suits in deep water. Some suits have their own built-in air supply so divers can breathe. One type has metal hands which can hold tools for working underwater. The diver in the picture is fixing an underwater cable.

What is an aqualung?

An aqualung is a small tank of air which a diver wears strapped to his back. A tube leads from the tank to the diver's mouth so he or she can breathe underwater. In the past, divers breathed air through a tube from a ship on the surface. It made moving about very difficult.

What is a submersible?

A submersible is a small craft like a mini submarine. Divers use submersibles for exploring the deep sea and searching for shipwrecks. Submersibles are also used to study life at the bottom of the ocean.

Deep-sea divers sound like Mickey Mouse.

TRUE. One of the gases deep-sea divers breathe makes their voices sound high-pitched and very squeaky.

Submarines can dive to the bottom of the sea.

FALSE. Submarines can only dive to about 700 m. The Pacific Ocean is about 11,000 m deep.

What are mermaids?

In olden days, sailors told stories of mermaids on rocks in the sea. The mermaids were women with fishes' tails. Legend said that if a sailor caught a mermaid, she would grant him three wishes in return for setting her free.

What is the Bermuda Triangle?

For centuries, ships and planes have mysteriously vanished in the Bermuda Triangle in the Atlantic Ocean.

?*Where is the city of Atlantis?*

No one really knows. Legend said that Atlantis was an ancient city on an island in the Atlantic Ocean. Its people were very rich and powerful. Then, one day, the island sank and no trace of it has ever been seen.

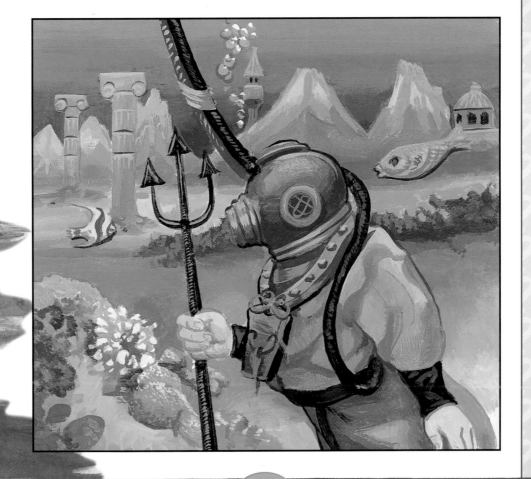

Why are sunsets orange?

and other questions about weather

What makes the weather change?

What's the weather like today? Is it sunny or rainy, windy or calm? There are few countries where the weather doesn't change from day to day, or week to week. The weather is blown around the world by powerful winds – which is why a change in the wind often brings a change in the weather!

Why does the wind blow?

Wind is moving air, and air moves when it warms up. This is because warm air is lighter than cold air, so it rises – that's why hot-air balloons float up into the sky. When warm air floats up into the sky, cold winds flow in to take its place.

How does the Sun drive the weather machine?

There would be no weather without the Sun. As it beams down on the Earth, the Sun warms the land and the oceans, and they give off heat which warms the air above them. Some parts of the world get hotter than others, and these differences in temperature create the powerful winds that blow the weather around our planet.

Average world temperatures. Warmest temperatures shown in dark colours, coolest temperatures shown in light colours.

What is the atmosphere?

The atmosphere is the thin skin of air which surrounds and protects our planet Earth. The air is a mixture of invisible gases – the main ones are nitrogen and oxygen.

Space

Northern lights

Shooting stars

Ozone layer

Weather

Earth's surface

Where is the ozone layer?

There's only a tiny amount of ozone gas in Earth's atmosphere, but it's very, very important. It forms a thin layer about 30 km above the ground, where it works rather like sunblock, protecting us from the Sun's harmful light rays.

❓ *Why is sunlight dangerous?*

The Sun's harmful rays are called ultraviolet light, and although we can't see them, they're powerful enough to burn and blister skin. Sunblock creams protect us from the Sun's ultraviolet light, so if you're outdoors during the summertime, make sure you slap on some cream and slip on a hat.

? How do scientists forecast the weather?

Scientists use special instruments to collect information about the Earth's atmosphere. All the information is fed into powerful supercomputers, which work out what is likely to happen to the weather and produce the kind of weather maps you see on television.

? What are weather stations?

These are places where weather instruments record everything from how fast the wind is blowing, and from which direction, to the temperature and the moisture in the air.

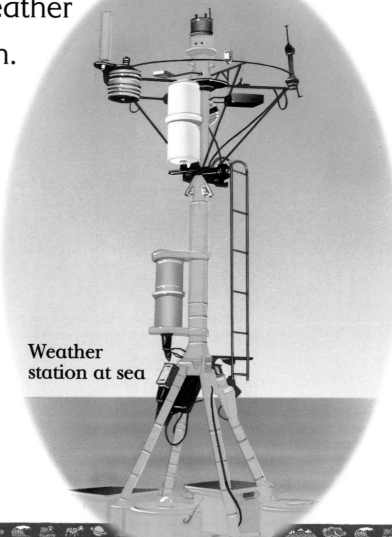

Weather station at sea

Snoopy

?Who is Snoopy?

Weather planes also fly high above the Earth. Some kinds are nicknamed Snoopy because they snoop out information with the weather instruments in their long pointy noses. Weather information is also gathered by instruments on ships at sea and satellites out in space.

TRUE OR FALSE?

Weather forecasts are always correct.

FALSE. Forecasts for the next 12 to 24 hours are usually correct, but not always! Long-term forecasts are far less likely to be correct.

Pine cones can predict the weather.

TRUE. If you hang one up outside, it will open in dry weather, and close when rain is on the way.

？What are clouds made of?

Clouds are made of billions of water droplets or ice crystals, which are so tiny and light that they float in the air. They come from an invisible gas called water vapour, which turns into water droplets when it cools. If the air is really cold, it freezes into ice crystals.

What is fog?

Walking through fog is rather like drifting through a cloud. That's because fog is also made up of tiny water droplets. Unlike clouds, though, fog forms just above the ground.

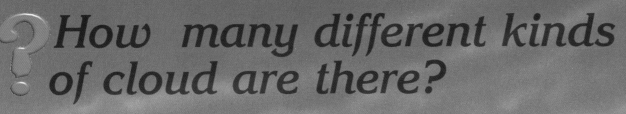

How many different kinds of cloud are there?

Scientists divide clouds into three main groups, with names that describe their shape.

Cirrus clouds are wispy and curly, and they're the highest clouds. Stratus clouds form in layers or sheets – some close to the ground, but others, called altostratus, higher up (alto means 'high').

Fluffy, heaped-up clouds are called cumulus.

Cumulus clouds

Stratus clouds

Cirrus clouds

Altostratus clouds

TRUE OR FALSE?

A mackerel sky is named after a fish.

TRUE. With its ripples and waves of high cumulus clouds, the sky is patterned like the markings on a mackerel fish.

Earth is the only planet with clouds.

FALSE. Other planets that have clouds include Venus, Jupiter, Uranus and Neptune.

❓ Can clouds tell us about the weather?

They certainly can. Small fluffy cumulus clouds are a sure sign of fine weather. Get your umbrella out if you see high cirrus or altostratus clouds – there's probably rain on the way. A blanket of stratus clouds usually brings drizzle.

❓ Which are the tallest clouds?

Thunderclouds are huge black stormclouds which can tower 18 km into the sky. That's more than twice as high as Mt Everest!

Scientists call thunderclouds cumulonimbus.

❓ What is lightning?

A flash of lightning is a gigantic spark of electricity which zips from cloud to cloud, or down to the ground, during a thunderstorm. Lightning is so hot that it heats the air until it booms – with a deafening clap of thunder.

Lightning is hotter than the Sun's surface.

TRUE. Lightning reaches 33,000°C – over five times hotter than the Sun's surface.

Lightning never strikes twice in the same place.

FALSE. New York's Empire State Building was once struck 15 times in 15 minutes!

? *Why do we see lightning before we hear thunder?*

We see lightning first because light travels much more quickly than sound. You can tell how far away a storm is by counting the seconds between a lightning flash and the thunder. Divide by three to get the number of kilometres.

Why does it rain?

Raindrops form inside clouds, as water droplets bash into each other and cling together, getting bigger and heavier. The water droplets carry on growing until they're too heavy to float in the air, and they fall to the ground as rain.

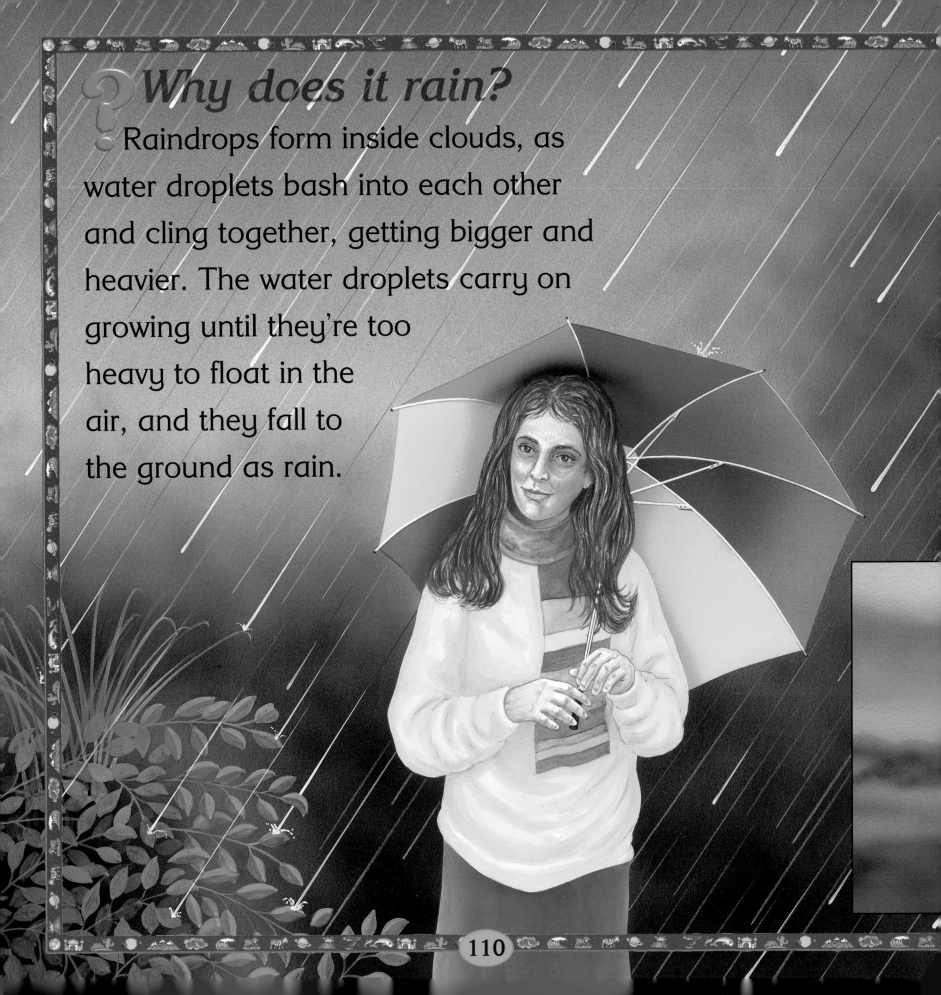

?*When do rainbows form?*

Rainbows are so magical because they only form when we have sunshine and rain – two things that hardly ever happen in the same place at the same time. The Sun's light may look white, but it's actually made up of all the colours of the rainbow – red, orange, yellow, green, blue, indigo (violet-blue) and violet. Raindrops split sunlight into all its different colours, and we see a beautiful curving rainbow.

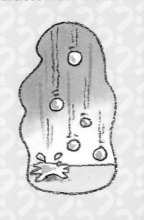

Why is the sky blue?

White light can be made from red, green and blue light.

As sunlight travels towards the Earth, it has to pass through the atmosphere. The atmosphere scatters some of the rainbow colours of sunlight much more than the others. Violet, indigo, blue and green are scattered the most, and they mix together to turn the sky blue.

Why are sunsets orange?

The Sun is low in the sky at sunset or sunrise, and sunlight has to travel farther through the atmosphere to reach us. Yellow, orange and red are scattered the most, mixing into a fiery orange.

What turns the sky grey?

Have you ever mixed all the colours in a paintbox together and ended up with a muddy grey? That's what happens when the sky is cloudy.

All the colours of sunlight are scattered and mix together.

❓ What are seasons?

In many parts of the world, the climate changes during the year. These changes are called seasons. Winter is the coldest, when many trees lose their leaves. Spring brings new growth, followed by the hottest season, summer. Autumn weather is cooler, then it's winter again.

Winter   Spring

Dried riverbed

❓ Where are there only two seasons?

In some tropical lands, there are only two seasons. During the wet season, it can bucket down for months on end. During the dry season, there's so little rain that the ground can bake and crack open.

? *What is a monsoon?*

The monsoon is a seasonal wind that brings heavy rain to some tropical countries. In India, the monsoon lasts from June to September, and dumps nearly the whole year's rain.

Summer   Autumn

Monsoon

How cold is snow?

Snowflakes are made up of lots of tiny ice crystals, which form from water vapour when the temperature inside clouds drops to freezing point – O˚C. Like rain, snow falls when snowflakes get too big and heavy to float in the air.

Snowflakes

What is frost?

Sometimes when you open the curtains on a cold winter morning, it looks as though someone has painted the outside of the windows and all the plants outdoors with ice. This is frost, and it's actually frozen dew. Dew forms on clear, windless nights, when water vapour in the air near the ground cools into water. If the weather is cold enough, the dew freezes into frost.

What is hail?

Hailstones are lumps of ice which sometimes form inside thunderclouds. They begin as frozen raindrops or snow pellets, which grow bigger and heavier as they're tossed up and down inside the thundercloud. When the hailstones get too big to float in the air, they plummet like bullets to the ground.

Hailstones are made up of layer upon layer of ice, as this cutaway shows.

Hailstones can be as big as bowling balls.

TRUE. Most are pea-sized, but some can be much larger. One that fell in 1970 was as big as a tenpin bowling ball.

Antarctic penguins huddle together during blizzards.

TRUE. Antarctica has some of the world's worst blizzards, and penguins survive by cuddling up in big huddles.

❓ *How fast do blizzards blow?*

A blizzard is a blinding snowstorm whose winds blow at over 55 kph. And if that isn't bad enough, blizzard temperatures can drop to as low as minus 12°C – Brrrrr!

❓ *How strong are gale winds?*

In 1806, an English admiral called Sir Francis Beaufort worked out a scale of 0 to 12 for measuring the strength of the wind. On this scale, 0 means no wind. By 3, there's a gentle breeze and you can see branches moving. Full gale force is 10 or above – trees are uprooted and buildings are damaged.

Scientists use an instrument called an anemometer to measure wind speed.

Beaufort scale

1	2	3	4	5	6	7	8	9	10	11	12

? *What is a sandstorm?*

During a sandstorm, shrieking winds whip up sand from the ground and hurl it through the air in a scratching, choking cloud. These storms mainly happen in sandy deserts, but they can also happen along beaches or dry riverbeds.

?How fast do hurricanes spin?

Hurricanes are terrifying scale 12 storms, whose winds can whirl around faster than 300 kph. They form over warm ocean water, in tropical regions above and below the equator. Most stay out at sea, but if they hit the coast they can sweep away whole towns.

?Where is the eye of a hurricane?

The eye is a calm area in the middle of the hurricane, around which the storm winds howl and roar. It usually measures about 30 km across, while a big hurricane can be more than 500 km across.

Hurricane seen from space

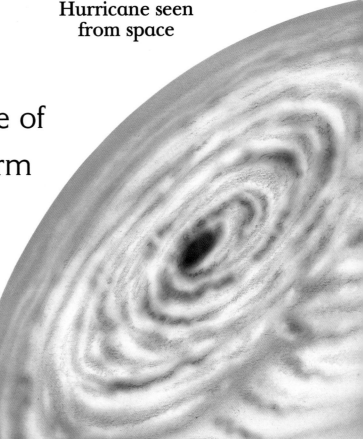

Unlike hurricanes, tornadoes form over land.

❓ *What's a twister?*

Some people call tornadoes 'twisters'. They're another kind of spinning storm, and although they're smaller than hurricanes, they can be even more violent. The heart of a tornado is like a giant vacuum cleaner, which sucks up everything in its path.

TRUE OR FALSE?

Gales howl more quickly than hurricanes.

FALSE. Even if they're powerful enough to uproot trees, gales don't blow much faster than 100 kph.

Tornadoes can spin faster than hurricanes.

TRUE. They can whizz around at over 480 kph.

What is clean energy?

Dirty, polluting gases are given off when coal and oil are burnt in power stations to generate electricity. Dirty gases are also given off by cars. But the natural world can give us power without pollution – this is clean energy.

Wind turbines are a clean way of generating electricity, They are powered by the natural energy of the wind.

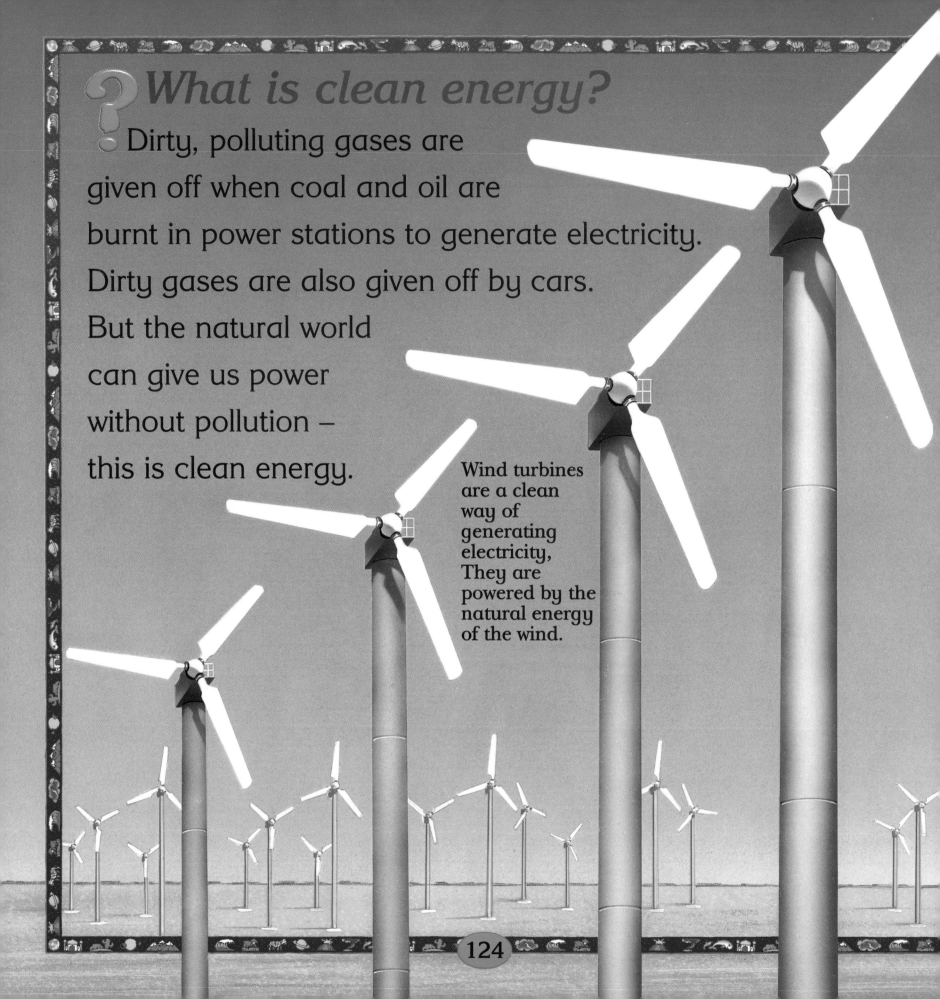

?How can we use the Sun's energy?

Sun power may drive the world's weather, but this uses only a tiny fraction of the Sun's heat and light energy. Solar panels are clever gadgets which capture the Sun's energy and turn it into electricity – without polluting the Earth's precious air and water.

Solar power station

Index